FUKUSHIMA DREAMS

poems by

Andrea Moorhead

Finishing Line Press
Georgetown, Kentucky

FUKUSHIMA DREAMS

Copyright © 2022 by Andrea Moorhead
ISBN 978-1-64662-925-1   First Edition
All rights reserved under International and Pan-American Copyright Conventions. No part of this book may be reproduced in any manner whatsoever without written permission from the publisher, except in the case of brief quotations embodied in critical articles and reviews.

ACKNOWLEDGMENTS

Inflectionist Review: "Fukushima Flees"
Osiris: "Fukushima Woman," "Letter from Fukushima," "Light over Fukushima," "Easter in Fukushima," "Before Fukushima"
Abraxas: "Silence from Fukushima," "Fukushima Remembers"
Indefinite Space: "Fukushima Forgets," "Fukushima Dreams"

Other Books by Andrea Moorhead:
Morganstall (Fiddlehead Poetry Books, 1971)
Entre nous la neige, correspondance québécaméricaine (Les Écrits des Forges, 1986)
Niagara (Écrits des Forges, 1988)
Le silence nous entoure (Écrits des Forges, 1991)
Winter Light (Oasis Books, 1994)
La blancheur absolue (Écrits des Forges/Autres Temps, 1995)
From A Grove Of Aspen (University of Salzburg Press, 1997)
Le vert est fragile (Écrits des Forges/Autres Temps, 1999)
Présence de la terre (Écrits des Forges, 2004)
De loin (Éditions du Noroît, 2010)
Terres de mémoire (Éditions de l'Atlantique, 2012)
Sans miroir (Encres Vives, 2013)
Géocide (Éditions du Noroît, 2013)
À l'ombre de ta voix (Éditions du Noroît, 2017)
The Carver's Dream (Red Dragonfly Press, 2018)
Tracing the Distance (The Bitter Oleander Press, 2022)

Publisher: Leah Huete de Maines
Editor: Christen Kincaid
Cover Art: Robert Moorhead
Author Photo: Robert Moorhead
Cover Design: Elizabeth Maines McCleavy

Order online: www.finishinglinepress.com
also available on amazon.com

Author inquiries and mail orders:
Finishing Line Press
PO Box 1626
Georgetown, Kentucky 40324
USA

Table of Contents

Fukushima Flees 1

Fukushima Woman 2

Letter from Fukushima 3

Silence from Fukushima 4

Light over Fukushima 5

Fukushima Remembers 6

Fukushima Remains Silent 7

Easter in Fukushima 8

Fukushima Glows at Night 9

Fukushima Alone 11

Fukushima Two 12

Beyond Fukushima 13

Fukushima in September 14

Fukushima at the Winter Solstice 15

Fukushima Forgets 16

Fukushima Dreams 17

Fukushima Christ 18

Fukushima will never 19

Before Fukushima 20

Fukushima Winter 21

Fukushima Flees

Unknown ash above the maple
seeds from distant and evolving
but amazement unless and then uncertain
we are moving too swiftly to concentrate on the wind,
air displaced creates a ripple along the seam of the day
light shattering pupils and the only way to restore balance,
unknown ash is wavering along the horizon
glinting as snow on a sudden night
arms open to the darkness but catching on the branches
ever so fragile in the upper air.

Fukushima Woman

The snow fallen in your hair
creates a nest for the moon and stars,
its shadow casting delicate and imprecise,
the strands across skin without warmth
swaying as you watch, wait, wonder when and if
sun radiates so softly the skin shimmers
whispering in the twilight
two stark figures searching the waves.

Letter from Fukushima

It's raining over Fukushima
the water collects at the back door,
stones still line the walk glistening under the rain,
nothing glows here, it's all in the mind,
one flower in the spring snow
mauve sad in the softly flickering and
smooth-toothed solar wind,
I'm alone here, shadows everywhere
the scent of the wind glinting in my nostrils
no one else could remain by the back door watching
the waves recede
an angel pulling out as the dead pile up
and I'm an old man before the wind, the rain, the errant snow.

Silence from Fukushima

Someone is moving along the shore
as if suspended from the clouds
the sun's rays filtering through her hair
I haven't seen this mirage before
against the broken shattered,
but you can come with me now
the light is no longer heavy, the earth still,
the ocean carries its fire too high to avoid
but we'll take the other road and you'll see the woman coming,
suspended perhaps or has someone lifted her above
and then sent her backwards downwards until
she arrives at our door, bearing a scalding bouquet that glows in the twilight,
hint of eternal condemnation and the beauty of dying
transcends our fear.

Light over Fukushima

I'm still by the back door
alone as twilight or morning,
the bodies buried now, carried to a gentle earth
praying as we lift and settle in
that no one else and the light glowing around the trunk
sears the path of inquiry,
we cannot articulate this renewal now
the illusion is immense
and children cannot discover the fatality of waiting by the back door
while light burns all around and the sea heaves and twists,
gentle sparrows gather by your tomb,
I've put the only flowers I had by the side of the road
no one will come along to take them
they're all afraid of dying,
and the light wraps itself around my eyes
torching the only sight I've ever had
of this eternal and consistent
memory of dying.

Fukushima Remembers

Snow flowing and your arms
the only and eternal this pattern
on light moving,
the water is calm this evening and
flowing swiftly mauve green rose
and the figures on the shore entwined,
the thought of night coming
snow flowing and your arms
the only and eternal
light moving.

Fukushima Remains Silent

Fast patterns etched in mud, calligraphy from ancient books, the pages left at the rim and burning still as the scribes wander about, looking for clues, the script so fragile, our boots heavy, and the leaf veins remain, frail suns sliced by an ancient and forlorn but the seat of light on the head hands but hearts are wandering in the deep snow, elsewhere water runs radiant and lips blistered cannot form the words again, fast patterns etched in mud, calligraphy of other veins, other systems that we haven't touched again, ever since and forgotten the sweet distant and clear, burning lips sound the sea, can the mud survive our frantic, remain and simmer without disappearing as night or day washing the cavern and survival depended more on elocution than any attempt to retrace the infinite and fragile before our eyes.

Easter in Fukushima

My child will have no necklace
no bright assent of lambs
straying far from slaughter
no glistening along the eyelids
token of love or steadfast adherence to the land
these hooves have turned sideways
flowering and glowing as the night air remains
my child will have no necklace of pearls
no fragile beam from the undersea
while we float against the tide inert eternal
and the wooly lambs have escaped slaughter
left trace to follow and wonder as the daystar rises
impenetrable horror in the rain and snow
but stones have overturned and spontaneous
the door opens as if there were some other realm
and the white light on your eyes
blinded and blinding
this cannot be the source of the lamb's forgiveness
this awkward ascent to the highest peak
for here only there is shelter in touching the rain twice
before night crumbles and disintegration culls out the weakest
and hooves have left trace in the spring soil
wherever the rain cannot penetrate, flowers have grown
and my child will have no necklace of pearls
but the sweet sound of sun on the summit will call
this assenting movement grace,
the white and consenting halo
wandering the blood fields of eternal sleep
the necklace necessary to cleanse and lighten
poisoned flesh.

Fukushima Glows at Night

A young child remembered a drawing of goldenrod flowers
placed silently against a stone, pasture moving brown and white
it was somewhere far to the west, across the planet's tallest
mountains, the briny seas left to scorch and shrink, ground
beige and yellow stained, farther to the west, across sand and
fig plantations, across olive groves and vineyards, across the
fabled lands no one can ever find again, across islands so cold air
condenses in snow and steaming ground shakes and shivers but
the earth is not on fire here, smoldering, sinking, scouring out the
sky, farther still, across and then turning abruptly north, there are
soft fields somewhere to the north, gentle sun and snowing rain,
and the mist is soft yellow there, pleasing to the eye, warming
the heart as a young child remembered a drawing of goldenrod
flowers placed silently in an earthenware vase by the back door.

Fukushima Alone

A state of mind left behind at Fukushima
radiant skin and eyes scorched by water's transformation,
the path leading around the bay is intact
although no one could get close enough to take a picture
or sketch the soft sinuous and certain
curve of the land at night.

Fukushima Two

Reconstruction begins softly, the step uncertain
no one able to recall whether the light was ever sweet
and gentle, the rain ever clear ever cool and the wind mild nurturing
grass birds children, softly the step uncertain
slippery and deceptive the steep path climbs
and all the sides together have no edge
tonight walking softly surely against and all around
but the eyes still glow at the touch
and the heart blackened can never bleach out
the sound of the running sea.

Beyond Fukushima

Beyond Fukushima the sweet sound
of bells and children running against
the strong and pungent
sound of the sea racing high
the glass bells breaking on the beach,
there are no more priests walking out beyond the waves
no more hermits bringing in the wet salt blossoms
the moonflowers escaped, the still stinging fish from other stars
recalled whenever the days grow bright again
and softly ring across the rising tide.

Fukushima in September

The blue flowers you gathered yesterday
are still on the table
despite your absence.

Fukushima at the Winter Solstice

There's a lamb now in Fukushima, all soft furred and clean,
the children bring him flowers, delicate from the winter rain
miraculous as a wreath laid on the foaming sea, the glowing soil
the rain so haunting and the tiny creature accepts the night as calm
the day as a sphere luminous and kind,
the children bring him water rinsed by the stars
share the silken grass by his side
weaving on the edge of the pen
all the lost light gathered from a withered spring.

Fukushima Forgets

The soft sweet rain
patter of children early in the day
wandering as birds spread their feathers
as boats haul anchor
and the wind rises fragile and clear
the tint of solitary exploration
and the sound of a woman weaving
so far from fire
so far from the green bitter salt disturbed.

Fukushima Dreams

There's a burning in the soul not unlike
the silver fire invisible
the cloak and dagger performance
of the rain the wind the sun exploding too close to the nerves
the switching of sound from within
and the burning never ceases
not unlike the sound of leaves rustling in the blood
when the soil decays at one ten-billionth of a mega-second
and statistics have no reality while the light kindles unknown fires
and nervous eyes follow the snow to saturation,
skin glowing at night
to the sound of dreams scraping the sky bare.

Fukushima Christ

Bones exposed and the waves continue
burning out the fires
hollowing shaft of and echoing in
this cannot remain without attendance
burning words at the height of the disaster
eyes swimming into the air
only holding the sound of day
the sound of night
knowing the source has been scoured, detached, abandoned
and things cannot remain in this state,
you haven't spoken for hours
the only assurance of your presence
the steady beating at the window
the swing of light from west to east
particles without labels
maybe rain maybe dust
maybe the sound of your eternally open heart.

Fukushima will never

replace the sun
winter clings, the rage internal
blue-grey and switching directions
snowing eyes have burdened the night
left marks no one can read,
a syncopation of desire and bereavement
trailing along the wind.

Before Fukushima

Chains of pebbles burning along the shore
an impossible necklace soldered together,
hands unknown and washed in uranium
as if the face had no more countenance
than this slow upheaval of certainty
this encapsulation of fear
that earth will no longer
and centuries enshrouded
at the touch your trembling hands.

Fukushima Winter

Fukushima in the snow
the grey dust behind eyes and hearts,
the ground here is hard and cold
we can't strew enough green leaves
to gentle, soften, and stir the soil
and everywhere voices clatter along
proclaiming red cannot be silver or gold
and the sudden lapse in memory
is only the work of time,
waiting for the snow to melt along the ocean
where the soil glows at night
and skin wears an uneasy mantle
waiting for the dawn, for the sweet fragrance
of another age.

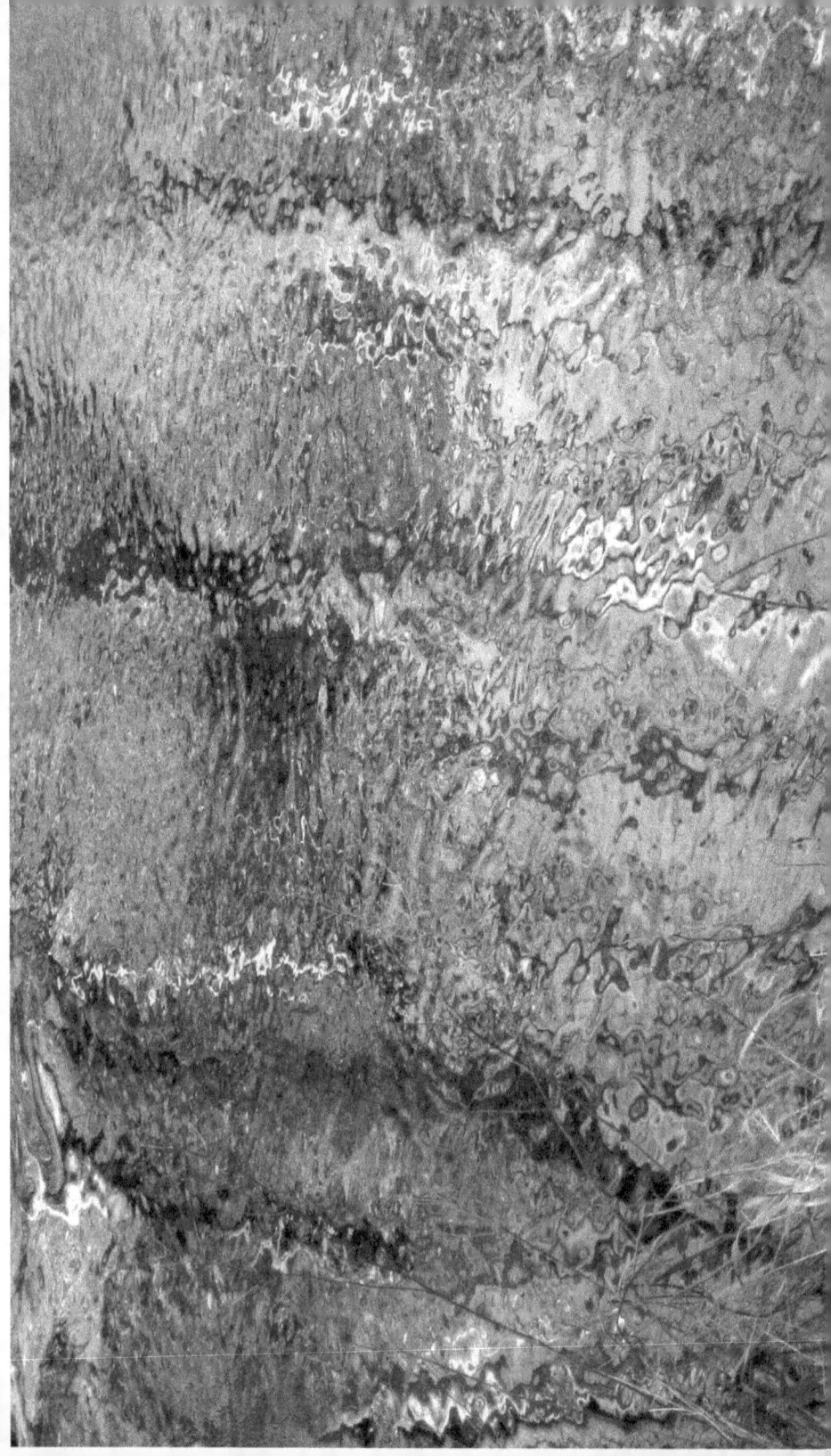

Book Translations by Andrea Moorhead:

The Edges of Light, selected poems of Hélène Dorion (Guernica Editions, 1995)
The Caverns of History, Hélène Dorion (Éditions en Forêt /Verlag Im Wald, 1996)
Do Not Disclose This Word, Jean Chapdelaine Gagnon (Spectacular Diseases, 1997)
Updates, Françoise Hàn (Éditions en Forêt / Verlag Im Wald, 1999)
Bridges, Dust, Hélène Dorion (Éditions en Forêt /Verlag Im Wald, 2000)
Night Watch, Abderrahmane Djelfaoui (Red Dragonfly Press, 2009)
Stone Dream, Madeleine Gagnon (Guernica Editions, 2010)
Dark Menagerie, Élise Turcotte (Guernica Editions, 2013)
The Red Bird, Marie-Christine Masset (Éditions Oxybia, 2020)

Andrea Moorhead was born in Buffalo, New York, in 1947, and lived there until 1962 when the family moved to the New York metropolitan area. Her early personal geography included the Niagara River, the beauty of its shores and the impact of petro-chemical installations on the environment, the beaches of Lake Erie, and the Muskoka Region north of Toronto. At an early age, Moorhead developed a keen sense of place, which would later play a significant role in her writing.

Her earliest poems were lyrical, somewhat hermetic, and imagistic. In time, language became almost a musical hammer to break out a series of complexly interwoven motifs. The context ontological, the language sensual. Moorhead's poems often develop multiple voices that interact. Sometimes it is the Earth that speaks, sometimes a person. The interplay between different voices creates dynamic tension in the poems and allows the reader to participate on many levels.

Over the years, Moorhead has incorporated ecological concerns and world events in her writing. The impact of global conflicts, natural disasters, and human destructiveness has become an important aspect of her work. The impact of wars and climatic extremes on people's lives is the focus of poems that move the reader towards the transcendent nature of the human spirit. *Fukushima Dreams* celebrates the spirit of Fukushima that absorbs and overcomes the tragedy of the March 2011 nuclear disaster.

www.ingramcontent.com/pod-product-compliance
Lightning Source LLC
LaVergne TN
LVHW041519070426
835507LV00012B/1679